D0633238

dude
food

recipes for the modern guy

dude

Karen Brooks, Gideon Bosker,

food

and Reed Darmon

CHRONICLE BOOKS
SAN FRANCISCO

Design by Reed Darmon

Library of Congress Cataloging-in-Publication Data:

Brooks, Karen.
Dude Food: recipes for the modern guy/ by Karen Brooks, Gideon Bosker, and Reed Darmon.
        p.   cm.
ISBN 0-8118-1679-6 (hardcover)
1. Cookery.   I. Bosker, Gideon.
      II. Darmon, Reed. III. Title.
TX652.B68   2000
641.5—dc21   99-40022
                                          CIP
Printed in Singapore.

Distributed in Canada by
Raincoast Books
9050 Shaughnessy Street
Vancouver, British Columbia V6P 6E5

10 9 8 7 6 5 4 3

Chronicle Books LLC
85 Second Street
San Francisco, California 94105

www.chroniclebooks.com

Dedication

To the coolest dudes:
George, Alan, and Alex; Craig,
Jason, Brett, and Gavin;
Morty and Jay; and Jory and Rob
(and the women who eat
their cooking).
— Karen Brooks

To my daughter,
Bianca Lencek Bosker.
— Gideon Bosker

contents

when dude meets food

In the beginning, there was rack of lamb. God told Abraham to come up to the mountain with his son Isaac for a food fest. What the boss wants, the boss gets, even if it means cooking up a favorite son. As they lumbered up the trail, Isaac asked his father, "What's for dinner?" To which Abraham said, "You, my son, well done — consider it a small sacrifice." Isaac looked puzzled, not knowing God had requested Abraham to sacrifice him as a sign of loyalty to the divine power.

Abraham wanted to make good on this promise, so he took out a knife and was about to skewer Isaac, when he looked up to the heavens and yelled: "Whoa there, dude. I got something you're going to like a whole lot better."

And there, tangled in the bushes, appeared a young, meaty ram. Abe slapped the ram onto the grill, added some rosemary and thyme, and invited God to come on down for some incredible lamb. This was recorded history's first dude food moment, with all the requisite components: important guests for dinner, fresh, free-range ingredients, spur-of-the-moment entertaining, quick prep time, and male bonding at its divine best.

But that's only part of the story. The roots of masculine gastronomy also can be traced to Neanderthal man, who cooked his prey in open fire pits. A gradual evolution took men to the open range, then onto patios, and finally, in its most absurd manifestation, on top of their car engines. After millennia of fine-tuning, this tradition now finds its culmination in the tile-lined kitchens of sprawling metropolises, where modern men adjust the settings of blenders, gas-fueled grills, and microwave ovens to feed family and friends.

But let this not diminish the impulses that gave rise to dude food, as New York chef Anthony Bourdain outlined in *The New Yorker* (1999): "It was the unsavory side of professional cooking that attracted me in the first place. . . . I wanted it all: the cuts and burns on the hands and wrists, the ghoulish kitchen humor, the free food, the pilfered booze, the camaraderie that flourished within rigid order and nerve-shattering chaos. I would climb the chain of command from *mal carne* (meaning 'bad meat,' or 'new guy') to chefdom — doing whatever it took until I ran my own kitchen and had my own crew of cutthroats, the culinary equivalent of *The Wild Bunch*."

The allure of cooking has always had a special place in a man's heart. It's much more than bringing home the bacon and cooking it up for the table. Dude food is a way of life, freely interpreted, a life in which confidence, fearlessness, and fun metamorphose into truth and soul, guy-style. And while part of that gestalt is eating good food, the other part is knowing how to make it.

But guy truth is not found in starched white vestments and toques as tall as skyscrapers. The real tell is the refrigerator: Is it barren but for that half a six-pack and leaky carton of leftover *pad thai* takeout? Or is it sparsely but smartly provisioned with long-shelf basics that, with zero notice and all of five minutes' thought, allow you to throw a dinner party for four on a work night? Buck up, pal. Your name needn't be Wolfgang Puck to pull off the Big Culinary Lebowski, and with a few kitchen moves, some home-run recipes, and inside tips on setting the mood, you will find a gustatory and social magic that's hard to dispel.

The savvy male knows the rules of the game, makes the best of home-field advantage, and has a kitchen wired to cook for the five types of essential guests: the folks from work, parental figures, a love interest, flavor-phobic kids, or a pack of party animals with the caloric requirements of a sumo wrestling team. Put simply, a food dude is up to the challenge of cooking for anyone anytime, especially the person with power over his paycheck or, more important, his heart.

Dude Food is organized in chapters pegged to gastronomic rituals and events, from intimate dinners and barbecues to casual meals and holiday feasts, each with a bag of tricks and emergency maneuvers for men who find themselves in the driver's seat. Let the menu fit. Are your guests prospective in-laws fresh in from New York's Little Italy? (You Go, Risotto). Downtown gallery rats and courthouse sharpshooters? (The Ultimate Caesar). The Epic Love who dreams, impossibly, in Jung? (hello, Candlelight Caviar Omelet).

It's no secret that guys can be short in the patience department. Less is more, and shorter is better in the world of testosterone cuisine. For a species that likes to go from zero to sixty miles per hour in less than five seconds, this usually means preparing dishes with maximum performance using minimal effort. That's why these recipes play it lean and simple. But sometimes it takes a few extra miles to push a dish into the realm of the sublime. Live with it.

This means downshifting into a take-charge, "no *problema*" attitude that is at the very heart of dudeness. You can cook a wide range of dishes if you approach the grill or marinade bowl in the right frame of mind. A food dude always exhibits complete control and confidence, serving up cheese-dripping nachos with the same *je ne sais quoi* as swank pears poached in port.

Gastronomy, as Bourdain points out, is the science of pain. As he sees it, the male chef belongs to "a secret society whose ancient rituals derive from the principles of stoicism in the face of humiliation, injury, fatigue, and the threat of illness." The guys who run a "tight, well-greased kitchen are a lot like a submarine crew. Confined for most of their waking hours in hot, airless, spaces, and ruled by despotic leaders, they often acquire the characteristics of poor saps who were press-ganged into the royal navies of Napoleonic times — superstition, a contempt for outsiders, and a loyalty to no flag but their own."

Male cuisine is not a high falutin' but a high salutin' approach to cooking, in which men indicate with a flyboy's thumb's up sign that their mission has been accomplished. His royal dudeness of foodness is always up for cooking a meal, and victory is the ultimate goal. While guys may be tough on the outside, they are a nurturing breed that knows a great meal is a surefire way to win over the hearts and stomachs of friends, loved ones, and working companions.

Man's relationship to food is perhaps best expressed in the film *Big Night* (1996). Here, two immigrant brothers gamble their meager savings on a passion for food and a restaurant that makes an artful lunge for the American dream. In a make-or-break proposition, they painstakingly prepare a Byzantine feast for a "big" night to mark their debut on the New Jersey dining scene.

But when only a few friends show, the brothers are crushed . . . and penniless. As the night draws to a somber close, they rendezvous in the kitchen. To lift the veil of despair, the older brother cracks a few eggs into a bowl, whips them furiously with some spices, and then pours the contents into a hot skillet. After a few hiss-filled moments, they sit down for a heart-to-heart, and dig in.

A humble cloud of a perfect omelet is no match for the culinary *tour de force* the brothers choreographed earlier in the evening. But this simple, decisive, compassionate act of food preparation restores their faith in life and captures the essence of dude cuisine: a culinary creation born of inspiration and improvisation, in which a few cooking steps and a few key ingredients come together to produce a profoundly soul-comforting meal.

Whatever your reasons for cooking — commiserating with friends, wowing prospective conquests, heroically trying to win over the littlest palates — a few basic principles will get you through the tough times: Use fresh ingredients whenever possible; fork over the extra money for top-notch basics, such as imported Parmesan or good olive oil; size may not matter but quality really does.

At its best, male cooking makes a statement that spotlights a single flavor or food, from salmon to exotic mushrooms, ribs to chocolate chip cookies. From this intensity of focus derives another guiding principle: Too many flavors do spoil the broth. Even though bold cuisine is a marker of dudeness, one of the objectives of this book is to take men from the world of crude, rude food into the world of mood food, where nuance plays an important role.

Still, for most guys, subtlety is much less important than drama. It may be the turbocharge of a chocolate cake, the glory of Cognac-flamed

home fries, or the primal gratification of sizzling meat on the backyard grill. Whatever the object of a man's culinary obsession, we've noticed a tendency to pull out all the stops and shift into gastronomic overdrive, whether it be in the heat, sweet, or meat department.

The modern guy has come a long way from the defiant end of the food chain, though we're certain you'll still enjoy our Bad-Boy Burgers smeared with garlic mayo. But who would have guessed that mangos and portobellos would one day be food for a fella, or that takeout chow mein would give way to pasta glazed with butter and sage; that salami and ham would give way to rosemary and lamb?

Men are frequently recruited to prepare food that will sustain, seduce, excite, or energize hungry people. The recipes in this book are designed to give guys the tools they need. When asked to cook a meal, regardless of time, place, or company, just remember to flash that winning smile, give a thumb's up, and bark "Can dude!"

GIDEON BOSKER
KAREN BROOKS

dudes and don'ts

dudes:

1. Get psyched by studying the recipe at least a day before you plan to serve it. Visualize its presentation.

2. Are like architects: They have all the ingredients on hand to build the menu dish but don't hesitate to improvise if the project runs into problems.

3. Always have these essentials on hand for spontaneous meals with flair: kosher salt for best flavor; peppercorns for the pepper mill; lemons; high-quality olive oil; balsamic vinegar; unsalted butter; eggs; several dried pastas, including unusual-shaped Italian imports; ravioli and pot stickers in the freezer; good canned tomatoes; baking potatoes; fresh garlic; the best Parmesan cheese (a chunk of Parmigiano-Reggiano); a reliable barbecue sauce; a jar each of black (whitefish) and red (salmon) "caviar"; some fine chocolate; an inexpensive white wine for cooking; chilled Champagne; and a respectable bottle of Cabernet or Merlot.

4. Always have charcoal on hand. You never know when a lazy weekend afternoon will turn into a backyard grill-o-rama.

5. Have a six-pack in the fridge, a good bottle of Scotch, six cigars, and a pound of Sumatran coffee.

6. Have a kitchen tool box with the following: a few sharp, top-notch knives, including a paring, a 10-inch, and a serrated bread slicer, plus a sharpening steel; a garlic press; a swivel-bladed vegetable peeler; a lemon zester; a pepper mill; tongs; wooden spoons for stirring (they don't get hot); a spatula for nonstick pans; a wire whisk; a grater; and a colander.

7. Shell out for a handful of essential pans and equipment, including: a cast-iron skillet (9- or 10-inch), known for great heat distribution; two heavy-bottomed saucepans (2-quart and 4 1/2-quart) for simmering, saucing, and risotto action; an 8-quart heavy-bottomed, nonstick stockpot for soups, chili, and pasta; a heavy-bottomed nonstick sauté pan (11- or 12-inch) with a lid; a roasting pan with a roasting rack; a blender or food processor.

8. Have the basics for mixing and baking: Mixing bowls; measuring cups and spoons; one or two cookie sheets; a pie pan (metal or glass); an 8-inch baking pan; a rubber spatula; a rotary beater, manual or electric; an oven thermometer (essential for checking the accuracy of the heat control).

9. Keep a diverse selection of dried herbs and spices on hand and know how to use garlic, chiles, and other seasonings to enhance the flavor of dishes.

10. Understand the power of fresh herbs, including rosemary, basil, and sage, and know the world of difference between the flavor of flat-leaf (Italian) parsley and the ubiquitous curly leafed variety.

11. Have one kick-ass hot sauce that will rock your world.

don't :

1. Be a rude dude. If you are hosting a meal don't order in something a raving hyena wouldn't deign to sniff at. Just cook it — or have it catered.

2. Be a sub-dude who uses paper plates, plastic utensils, or disposable glasses for a party. Rent, borrow, or bargain for decent dishes, flatware, and glasses.

3. Let dates or guests get a glimpse of the slob you really are. Hire someone to do the pre- and post-cleanup.

4. Do all your food shopping at a convenience store.

5. Get into the checkout counter if your shopping cart has enough glass and metal to build a small skyscraper — too many cans and jars means not enough fresh ingredients.

6. Be a culinary crude dude. Don't buy Spam, beef jerky, honey-glazed ham, or frozen French fries.

7. Be a stewed dude. Do not inflict measurable liver damage on yourself as long as you are the host at the cocktail party.

8. Think party punches and kegs cut it after college. Bone up on microbrews and nail down a couple of savvy cocktails.

9. Be an aesthetic thug who sets a romantic table with plastic flowers, fresh carnations, or stinky daisies. Think tulips, roses, lilies, or orchids.

10. Put Tabasco sauce on everything.

11. Listen to Barry Manilow while cooking serious barbecue.

12. Talk to your broker, mother-in-law, or ex-lover while you're cooking.

13. Use your smoke alarm as a timer to indicate your roast is done.

14. Be a blue dude. Make time to invite your friends over for social occasions that involve good eating and conversation.

romancing

chapter 1
the stove

More than the final frontier, more than the elusive winning season, even more than searching for the ultimate wheels, a guy invariably struggles with the Big Question: How do I impress my date? The answer can't be found in some remote Tibetan canyon or deep in the books of love. The best way to get the desired effect is to create a dish of desire. Our midnight omelet, Cognac-splashed steak, and steamy dumplings come with no guarantees. But these intimate recipes offer inspiration for anyone burning to woo and chew. Remember, the best icebreakers are cocktails and compliments. And nothing beats dancing in the dark.

The Menu

- Love Me Tenderloin
- Fool-Proof Pasta (for fools in love)
- Thai Me Up Dumplings
- A Nice Piece of Bass
- Candlelight Caviar Omelet
- French Kiss

love me tenderloin

If you want to talk about relationships, then you've got to address the dance of a man and his steak. This is the inner ring of your psyche, the one indestructible primordial link to your Neanderthal roots. When a man shares his beef, he bares his soul. Call it instant intimacy on the table. Our pan-seared beef gets right to the meat of the matter. The buttery Cognac sauce adds the swoon factor of an Elvis replay, and a side order of the Ultimate Caesar (page 80) will provide that lusty garlic thrust.

- 1 tablespoon olive oil
- 4 tablespoons unsalted butter
- 2 beef tenderloin filet steaks, each 1 inch thick
- 2 green onions, minced
- 1/4 cup chicken broth (canned is okay)
- 1/2 cup Cognac
- Salt and freshly ground pepper

1. Heat the olive oil and 1 tablespoon of the butter in a nonstick skillet over medium-high heat. When hot, sauté the steaks, about 4 minutes on each side for medium-rare. Transfer the steaks to a plate, and keep them warm under a foil tent.

2. Pour any fat out of the skillet. Return the skillet to the stove and add 1 tablespoon of the butter. When the butter melts, add the green onions and quickly sauté. Add the broth and boil it down by one-half, 2 to 3 minutes, stirring to scrape up any bits from the bottom of the skillet. Add the Cognac, and boil rapidly 1 to 2 minutes to burn off the alcohol. Season with salt and lots of pepper.

3. Remove the skillet from the heat and swirl in the remaining 2 tablespoons of butter, a half table-spoon at a time. Add the steaks and turn once to coat both sides with the sauce.

4. Transfer the steaks to plates and top with any remaining sauce. Serve hot.

Serves 2

fool-proof pasta (for fools

Having a date over for dinner can let loose all kinds of rejection fears. The trick is confidence, the sense that within a matter of hours you can go from kitchen schlepper to Chez Dude! The secret is in the sauce. And by a fortunate fluke of chemistry, the combination of shredded lemon rind and white wine fired up in a saucepan with vivid cheese becomes — in five minutes — something right out of a Marseilles bistro. Use the best ingredients you can afford — organic lemons, crème fraîche (a blue-chip sour cream) and exceptional pasta, dried or fresh. Then sit back and relax, Pierre.

in love)

- 8 ounces pasta
- 3 lemons, washed
- $^1/_3$ cup dry white wine
- $1^1/_2$ tablespoons butter
- 1 small portobello mushroom, sliced
- $^1/_2$ cup crème fraîche or sour cream
- $1^1/_4$ cups (3 ounces) grated Gruyere cheese
- Salt and freshly ground pepper

1. Bring a large pot of salted water to a boil. Add the pasta and cook until al dente, with a slight resistance to the bite.

2. Meanwhile, with a hand grater or special "zesting tool," carefully grate the "zest" or rind (the thin, colored yellow part only; the white pith below is bitter) from the lemons. Measure out enough to generously fill a $^1/_4$-cup measure. Juice one of the grated lemons and set aside. Discard or save the others for another use.

3. Bring the grated lemon rind and wine to a boil in a large saucepan. Boil gently until the wine is reduced by a third, about 4 minutes.

4. Meanwhile, melt the butter in a skillet over medium heat. Add the mushroom slices and sauté until tender, about 5 minutes.

5. Drain the pasta and transfer it to the saucepan, mixing it with the grated lemon and wine mixture. Add the crème fraîche or sour cream and grated cheese, stirring briskly to combine. Season to taste with salt, pepper, and the reserved lemon juice. Serve in warm bowls topped with the mushroom slices.

Serves 2

thai me up dumplings

You're sitting on the couch, and you've hit that clumsy conversational impasse. But this is a hot date, and you want to keep the action happening. Face it: You've got to be cultured no matter how much it kills you. A little ethnic food savvy to the rescue. Just saunter over to the kitchen and pull out that bag of Asian dumplings or pot stickers you were smart enough to stash in the freezer. Then, as though this is an everyday event, casually whip together a spicy little peanut sauce while making small talk. "So, have you ever tried freshwater Mekong shrimp with baby bamboo shoots. No? Let me tell you about the time I was lost for three days in a Bangkok market . . ."

- 2 tablespoons balsamic vinegar
- 2 tablespoons Worcestershire sauce
- 2 heaping tablespoons creamy peanut butter
- 1 teaspoon minced garlic
- 1 teaspoon hot sauce
- 1 teaspoon sugar
- 12 frozen dumplings or pot stickers (see Note)
- 1 teaspoon vegetable oil

1. Combine all the ingredients except the dumplings and vegetable oil in a jar with a tightly fitting lid. Shake vigorously to blend. Taste and adjust the flavors. Transfer to a small serving bowl. Set aside.

2. Meanwhile, bring a pot filled with water to a boil; reduce the heat to a gentle simmer and cook the dumplings until tender, about 8 minutes. Drain the dumplings well to remove all the liquid.

3. Heat the oil in a nonstick skillet over high heat, swirling the oil to evenly distribute it. Pan-fry the dumplings until lightly golden, 1 to 2 minutes, flipping constantly with a spatula.

4. Transfer to a decorative plate and serve with the peanut sauce for dipping.

Makes 12 dumplings

NOTE: Frozen dumplings are available at Asian markets and some specialty grocery stores.

a nice piece of bass

This is the French connection to romance — provincial bait blended from parsley, butter, and garlic, smeared over delicate bass fillets, then broiled to sensuous glory. A few bites, and your date will be hooked. Serve with buttered rice, sliced tomatoes with fresh cracked pepper, and a fruity white wine. The fish can be prepped a few hours in advance and fired up just before serving. Experiment with other kinds of mild fish such as halibut, salmon, or cod. Play your lines right, and it's all downstream from here.

- 1 slice focaccia bread, about 5 inches wide and 2 inches thick; or 2 slices firm white bread
- 4 tablespoons unsalted butter, at room temperature
- 3/4 cup fresh flat-leaf (Italian) parsley
- 2 tablespoons fresh lemon juice
- 1 to 3 garlic cloves
- Salt and freshly ground pepper
- 2 to 3 teaspoons olive oil
- Three 6-ounce skinless sea bass fillets, each about 1 inch thick

1. Tear the bread into small pieces. Place all ingredients except the olive oil and bass fillets in a blender or food processor. Blend to a thick, smooth paste. Taste and adjust the flavors. Set aside.

2. Heat a large nonstick skillet over medium heat with enough of the oil to lightly coat the bottom of the pan. When the oil is hot, sear the fish on both sides for a few seconds, just enough to lightly brown each side. Be careful not to cook the fish through.

3. Carefully transfer the fish to a baking sheet. Spread 1 to 2 tablespoons of the paste evenly over the tops to create a top "crust."

4. When almost ready to serve, preheat the broiler to 500 degrees F (this can take up to 10 minutes); adjust the rack so it's in the top rung.

5. Broil the fillets until the top crust browns and the fish cooks through, 3 to 4 minutes. Serve hot.

Serves 3

candlelight caviar omelet

The electricity was unexpected but has turned seriously high voltage. You had always been warned to have that bottle of Champagne chilled and ready to go, and now you know why. You want to draw the moment out with a late-night love feast, something elegant and sexy. Question is: How to package a plate of romance on the spot? Eggs and caviar to the rescue. Just whip up an omelet and sprinkle on the legendary love beads. Present at once with the lovely French bread you bummed from the neighbor. Light candles. Spin Miles Davis. Pour some bubbly. Talk until the sun comes up.

- 3 large eggs
- 2 tablespoons water
- 1 teaspoon olive oil
- 1 heaping tablespoon butter
- 1 to 2 heaping teaspoons yogurt
- 1 heaping teaspoon black (whitefish) caviar
- 1 heaping teaspoon red (salmon) caviar

1. Crack the eggs in a mixing bowl. Add the water and beat until frothy.

2. Warm a skillet or omelet pan over medium heat. Add the olive oil and heat for 20 seconds or so. Then add the butter, whirling it around in the olive oil. After the butter has melted, when the foam begins to subside, the pan is ready for action. Add the eggs and, with a wooden spoon, move them about slightly, letting them firm without scrambling them.

3. When the eggs are no longer runny but still glisten, use a spatula to carefully fold one-third of the mixture over the center; repeat by folding the opposite third over the center. Cook another minute.

4. Transfer to a serving plate. Smear the top with yogurt, which creates a background to set off the caviar visually. Sprinkle the caviars over the yogurt, or build a caviar medallion — half red, half black.

Serves 2

the morning after
french kiss

The astute bachelor has a breakfast-in-bed strategy that includes serious coffee, freshly squeezed juice, perhaps with a little vodka to lubricate the conversation, and this secret French toast formula. The payoff is good for weeks. Our version uses rich, peel-apart butterflake rolls as the foundation for a sweet and smoldering apricot-orange sauce with glazed bananas. Look for the rolls at the supermarket bakery or substitute four slices of your favorite bread.

BATTER
- 3 large eggs
- $1/3$ cup milk
- $1/8$ teaspoon each: cinnamon, nutmeg, vanilla extract, and salt
- 4 butterflake rolls

SAUCE
- 2 tablespoons unsalted butter
- $1/2$ cup apricot preserves
- 1 teaspoon sugar
- $1/4$ cup orange juice
- 1 ripe banana, sliced

1. To make the batter: Combine all the batter ingredients except the butterflake rolls. Pour into a wide shallow dish. Peel the rolls into layers. Dip both sides in the batter to coat. Let soak in the batter 10 minutes, turning once after 5 minutes.

2. To make the sauce: Melt $1/2$ tablespoon of the butter in a saucepan over medium-high heat. Stir in the preserves, sugar, and orange juice. Cook until thick and caramelized but liquid enough to be poured, about 10 minutes, stirring occasionally. Add the banana slices, and cook until soft. Reduce the heat to low to keep the sauce warm.

3. Melt the remaining butter in a large skillet over medium-high heat. Cook the butterflake slices until golden brown, turning once. Serve hot with the sauce poured over the top.

Serves 2

male

chapter 2
bonding

When the boys get together, pretty tables and civilized pretensions don't factor. What counts is immediacy and intensity, food that allows for all kinds of latitude. This means dishes punched up with personality, the kind of culinary expressions you can throw together without calling your mom and then brag on when the guys show up. These get-together recipes go the distance, transforming classic guy grub like ribs and chili into statements high on style and low on maintenance.

The Menu

- Macho Nachos
- The Dagwood Deconstructed
- Big League Lamb Chili
- Four Men and a Baby Back Rib
- Heavy Mental Pot Roast

macho nachos

Think of this as a culinary poker game, playing for devilish beans and a hot hand of chips flush with chili powder, fresh lime, and sugar. The wild card here is the habanero pepper, a joker with a thermonuclear heart. Juice from the jar can amp a dish off the charts, and only a slightly maladjusted personality would eat one whole — that's why it's so much fun to call the bet. If habaneros are unavailable, season the beans with the juice from the can of sliced jalapeños.

- 1 small jar habanero peppers
- One 8-ounce can sliced jalapeño peppers
- Two 10-ounce cans spicy jalapeño refried beans
- 3^1/$_2$ cups salsa
- 2 tablespoons chili powder
- 1 tablespoon sugar
- 9 ounces plain tortilla chips
- Juice of 2 limes
- 1^1/$_2$ cups (6 ounces) shredded sharp cheddar or Monterey Jack cheese
- One 8-ounce container sour cream

1. Preheat the oven to 325 degrees F.

2. Drain the juice from the jar of habaneros or the can of sliced jalapeños into a bowl; set aside.

3. Heat the beans in a large nonstick skillet over medium heat, about 10 minutes, stirring occasionally. Stir in half the salsa. Add the reserved habanero or jalapeño juice, a little at time, tasting for the desired fire zone. Remove from the heat, and set aside.

4. Combine the chili powder and sugar. Put the chips in a large bowl, and toss with the lime juice and chili-sugar mixture.

5. Spread the bean mixture on a medium-size heat-proof tray (disposable aluminum ones are fine), working close to the rim and leaving a big hole in the middle. Pile half of the chips in the center, and cover with half of the cheese. Add the remaining chips and cheese. Bake until the cheese melts and the beans are hot, about 10 minutes.

6. Remove from the oven. Spoon the remaining salsa on top. Garnish with sliced jalapeños, sour cream, and whole habanero peppers — and let the best man win.

Serves 6 to 8

the dagwood deconstructed

This '50s idea of the ultimate sandwich was named after that comic strip Everyman, Dagwood Bumstead, who constructed the original mouth-stretching sub with sky-high layers of cold cuts and cheese. Our version goes postmodern with an architectural blend of Brie, fruit, and high-end ham, built with attention to form and color. Your neo-hipster pals will be impressed.

- 1 long crusty roll, 10 to 12 inches, sliced in half lengthwise
- 12 dried figs
- 8 ounces Brie, at room temperature
- 12 thin slices prosciutto or lean ham
- 8 thin slices deli turkey
- 8 thin slices smoked provolone cheese

1. Preheat the oven (or a toaster oven) to 350 degrees F.

2. Lightly toast the roll. Remove the stems from the figs, and thinly slice the fruit.

3. Spread half of the Brie over one toasted bread half. Build the sandwich vertically, beginning with a layer of half of the figs arranged over the Brie. Add all of the prosciutto or ham in a layer, overlapping the slices and folding each one in half. Add all of the turkey slices in a layer, then all of the provolone cheese slices. Top with a layer of the remaining figs.

4. Spread the rest of the Brie over the remaining toasted bread half, and close up the sandwich. Cut into slices to serve.

Serves 4

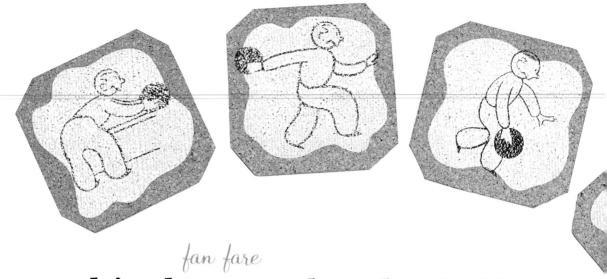

big league lamb chili

It's bone-wracking cold out there, and you've overhyped your kitchen moves to your bowling buds. Let's face it: You need a strike, and nothing else will do. That's where this chili comes in. It has attitude and flair, with black beans (instead of off-the-rack pintos), pungent lamb dressed in sun-zone spices, and points for uptown garnishes. Like all chili, this one is even better made a day in advance — after sitting overnight, the flavors really get some team chemistry. Leftovers can carry you through an entire play-off series: tossed into tortillas, scrambled up with eggs, or frozen in some wonder tub for a future chow-down.

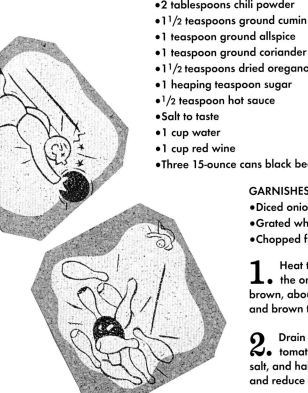

- 3 tablespoons oil
- 1 1/2 cups diced yellow onions (about 3 small onions)
- 4 garlic cloves, minced
- 1 1/2 pounds ground lamb
- Two 14 1/2-ounce cans diced tomatoes, with juice
- 2 tablespoons chili powder
- 1 1/2 teaspoons ground cumin
- 1 teaspoon ground allspice
- 1 teaspoon ground coriander
- 1 1/2 teaspoons dried oregano
- 1 heaping teaspoon sugar
- 1/2 teaspoon hot sauce
- Salt to taste
- 1 cup water
- 1 cup red wine
- Three 15-ounce cans black beans, drained

GARNISHES (any or all)
- Diced onions
- Grated white cheddar cheese
- Chopped fresh cilantro

1. Heat the oil in a large heavy pot over medium heat. Add the onions and garlic and sauté until the onions begin to brown, about 10 minutes. Add the lamb, break up the chunks, and brown the meat, about 10 minutes.

2. Drain the lamb mixture, and return it to the pot. Stir in the tomatoes, all of the spices, the oregano, sugar, hot sauce, salt, and half of the water. Stir in the wine. Bring to a boil, cover, and reduce the heat to simmer. Cook 1 hour.

3. Add the beans and remaining water to the pot. Cover and simmer 30 minutes, adding more water if the liquid evaporates. Taste and adjust the seasonings, pumping up the spices to hit the desired flavor zone.

4. Serve hot with bowls of garnishes on the side for toppings.

Makes 9 one-cup servings

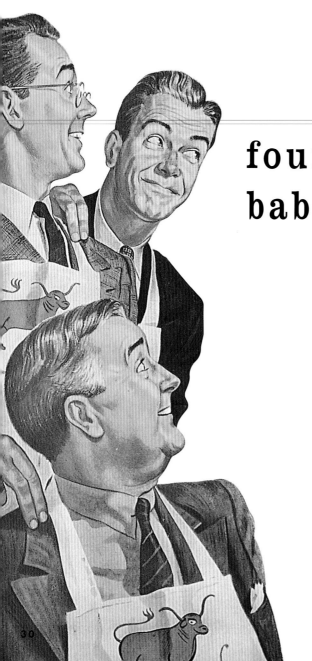

four men and a baby back rib

It's you, three buddies, and a night of serious bones and brew. Stash your dignity at the door, and get primitive with these pepper-blasted ribs rubbed down with brown sugar and roasted garlic. Bone-sucking animal grunts are encouraged. The challenge is to get through it all and still be in shape for some hip-hoppin' rhythm 'n' blues, along with our outrageous chocolate Beastie Bars (page 88). Be sure the coolerator is well stocked with enough mouth-chillin' beer to go the distance.

- 4 racks pork baby back ribs, each 1 1/4 pounds
- One 16-ounce bottle Italian salad dressing
- 6 teaspoons each: garlic powder and hot chili powder
- Salt and freshly ground pepper to taste
- 4 whole garlic heads, cut in half crosswise
- 1/2 cup olive oil
- 4 tablespoons dark brown sugar

1. An hour before you're ready to cook: Place the ribs in a single layer in a large roasting pan. Add the Italian dressing, and turn the ribs until well coated. Cover the pan with plastic wrap and refrigerate.

2. Preheat the oven to 325 degrees F.

3. Remove the ribs from the refrigerator. Sprinkle 1 teaspoon of the garlic powder, 1 teaspoon of the chili powder, and the salt and pepper evenly over the top of each slab.

4. Place the halved garlic heads in an ovenproof dish. Drizzle the oil evenly over the tops. Bake the ribs and garlic heads for 30 minutes. Remove the ribs from the oven and sprinkle 1 tablespoon brown sugar evenly over each rack. Bake 20 minutes. Remove from the oven. Sprinkle 1/2 teaspoon of the garlic powder and 1/2 teaspoon of the chili powder over each rack, then season generously with salt and pepper. Bake 20 minutes.

5. Increase the heat to 500 degrees F. If the garlic is soft enough to spread, remove from the oven. If not, cook along with the ribs another 10 minutes.

6. Serve the ribs hot along with the baked garlic on the side, so that it can be squeezed and spread over the tops.

Serves 4

heavy mental

It's the weekend, you've got intimacy fatigue, and the relationship is going nowhere. You need to connect with something. What could be better than home-style cooking and pals to share it with? So hunker down with a bottle of red, some great bread, and a *Spinal Tap* vid. Then bring on this hunky, fall-apart roast inspired by the basic four food groups: beer, chocolate, beef, and potatoes. Get going on the oven early in the day — you need to factor about three and a half hours in the cooker. Slice the leftover meat for some Prozacian BBQ beef sandwiches.

pot roast

- Two 1.4-ounce boxes onion soup mix, such as Knorr
- One 1.2-ounce package brown gravy mix, such as Knorr Classic
- $1/2$ cup brown sugar
- $1/2$ cup ketchup
- One pint strong dark stout, such as Guinness Extra Stout
- 1 square Mexican sweet chocolate, chopped (see Note)
- $3^1/4$ pounds beef pot roast
- 3 baking potatoes, quartered

1. Combine the onion soup mix, brown gravy mix, and brown sugar in a mixing bowl. Blend in the ketchup and stout. Let stand for 30 minutes. Add the chopped chocolate.

2. Meanwhile, preheat the oven to 325 degrees F.

3. Pour the stout mixture over the bottom of a roasting pan and add the pot roast, turning once to coat. Cover the pan tightly with aluminum foil. Bake 2 hours.

4. Remove the pan from the oven and turn the meat over. Add the potatoes and tightly recover the pan. Cook 2 hours, or until the meat is fork-tender. Remove the pan again and carefully pour off any liquid into a saucepan. Cover the roast and set aside.

5. Cook the liquid over medium-high heat until thick and gravylike, about 15 minutes, stirring occasionally.

6. Slice the meat and arrange on a platter with the potatoes. Pour 1 cup of the gravy on top. Serve extra gravy at the table.

NOTE: Mexican sweet chocolate is commonly found in the Mexican food section of many supermarkets and in Latin markets. If unavailable, substitute 1 square semisweet chocolate plus $1/4$ teaspoon cinnamon.

Serves 6

chapter 3

ceremonies

Sometimes you just need to be the top dog. Maybe it's a holiday, a birthday celebration, the solstice, or just an excuse to pull out the stops and experience the high life. These are precarious moments. You're investing time, money, and ego, so the plates better be up to snuff. The following centerpieces give you a range of moods to choose from — classic, inventive, and left-of-center. Keep the action going beyond the menu: Think real tablecloth, score some fresh flowers, and get a mood going with candles and tunes to fit.

The Menu

- Lusty Lamb

- You Go, Risotto

- Emergency Party Kit Pasta

- High-Rollin' Pasta with Lobster Sauce

- Peter's Principled Pork Tenderloin

- Jammin' Dishwasher Salmon

lusty lamb

Few entrées carry the weight, ritual, and time-lessness of lamb. Sadly, most guys believe its preparation is just as solemn and daunting, complicated by the procurement of embarrassing little paper crowns that fit over rib ends. Trade in your thinking on this one. This lamb is any-one's best culinary trick, built on the premise that a rack ruthlessly stripped of fat and scaled in herbed salt will cook quickly and evenly with dramatic result. It comes from the enlightened kitchen of our friend Len Reed. Know, for starters, what the big guys in the big kitchens have known for centuries: Roasting is less about fussing over the meat and more about the careful management of heat. If you can turn an oven dial exactly twice in a twenty-five-minute frame, you're home. Know, too, that rosy chops bring out the sybarite in everyone: The most elegant and formal of guests reliably drop their silver and go at these fragrant bones bare-handed. Mon dieu! Pass the Merlot — and a side of Len's Monster Mash potatoes (page 78).

- 2 racks of lamb, each about 1 1/2 pounds with 6 to 8 ribs
- 1/2 cup salt
- 1/2 cup dried thyme leaves
- 2 tablespoons freshly ground pepper

1. Hold a rack upright by grasping the rib ends with a paper towel. With a sharp knife carefully remove the thick fat layers covering the meaty side of the rack. The fat layer is thickest on top, and it helps to cut downward along the bone almost halfway, notching outward over the meat before continuing downward. Follow the contour of the meat, being careful not to pierce it or separate it from the bone, and pulling bits of fat away with your fingers if necessary. The goal is to remove as much fat as possible — about a third of the rack's weight in fat. Repeat the process with the second rack.

2. Preheat the oven to 450 degrees F.

3. Mix the remaining ingredients in a bowl. Place the racks on a cookie sheet or in a roasting pan. Apply the salt-herb mixture to all sides, pressing it into the meat with your hands. Reapply liberally, making sure all surfaces are well coated. Leave extra seasoning in the base of the pan to scent the meat — and the house.

4. Bake the racks, bone side down, for 12 minutes to shock-roast the meat, "fixing" the salt-herb mixture and sealing in juices. Open the oven door for a minute and reduce the heat to 325 degrees F. Roast 20 minutes for medium-rare, another 5 minutes for something less pink.

5. Remove from the oven and let the meat sit 5 minutes under a foil tent.

6. Stand the racks upright and slice between the bones to create 1/2-inch-thick chops. Reserve the juice from the cutting board and drizzle over the chops before serving.

Serves 4

you go, risotto

Every guy needs a signature dish, something that establishes his reputation, no matter how mismatched the silverware. And what could be better than this pinnacle of Italian cuisine: warm bowls of rice swollen in broth to an exquisite texture that is equal parts heaven and earth? This version includes a last-minute flavor pump of lemon and egg yolk. The technique is simple but extremely sensitive to time and heat, so pay attention. Italian arborio rice is shorter and thicker than American varieties, giving the dish more substance and bite and it's worth the search.

- 2 quarts best-quality, low-salt canned chicken broth
- 2 tablespoons unsalted butter or olive oil, plus an optional 2 more tablespoons of butter
- 1 medium yellow onion, minced
- 2 1/2 cups arborio rice
- Salt to taste
- 1 medium lemon, washed
- 1 large egg yolk
- 1/2 cup (2 ounces) grated Parmesan cheese, preferably Parmigiano-Reggiano

1. Bring the chicken broth to a boil in a saucepan. Reduce the heat to a simmer.

2. Heat the 2 tablespoons of butter or olive oil in a large heavy skillet over medium heat. Add the onion and sauté until translucent, about 3 minutes.

3. Increase the heat to high. Add the rice, stirring briskly, until the grains are translucent, about 1 minute. Reduce the heat to low and pour in enough of the simmering broth to barely cover the rice, stirring once or twice. Season with salt. Adjust the heat so the liquid is barely bubbling. When the surface forms little air pockets (about 2 minutes), stir in enough stock to barely cover the rice again. As the rice swells and absorbs the liquid, continue adding enough broth to barely cover the top. Add salt to taste on occasion. Cook until tender but still firm and creamy, 20 to 22 minutes from start to finish.

4. Meanwhile, grate the rind of the lemon (yellow part only). Juice the lemon. Whisk the lemon rind, lemon juice, and egg yolk in a small bowl.

5. When the rice is finished, remove the pan and slowly stir in the egg yolk mixture until thoroughly incorporated. Stir in the grated cheese. If the rice is too dry, add a little stock. Add the remaining 2 tablespoons of butter, if desired, for a richer texture. Serve immediately in very warm bowls.

Serves 4 to 6

emergency party kit pasta

Can't talk now . . . got to get moving on this impromptu feast of store-bought ravioli upgraded with basil, freshly cooked tomatoes, and toasted pine nuts. Pick up some greens for a simple salad, and serve with a heady red wine and a couple of pints of sorbet for dessert. Activate the cooking plan by chopping everything in advance. Once you fire up the skillet, the whole affair takes less than twenty minutes.

- 6 tablespoons olive oil
- 3/4 cup pine nuts
- Salt to taste
- Big pinch dried red pepper flakes
- 1/3 cup chopped garlic (1 small garlic bulb)
- 4 medium tomatoes, seeded and chopped
- Freshly ground pepper to taste
- 2 1/2 pounds fresh ravioli, ideally a mix of colors
- 1 cup chopped fresh basil
- 1 cup grated Parmesan cheese

1. Heat 2 tablespoons of the oil in a small skillet over medium-high heat. Sauté the pine nuts until light golden brown, 2 to 3 minutes. Remove from the heat, season with salt, and set aside in a bowl.

2. Heat the remaining oil and the red pepper flakes in a 3 1/2-quart saucepan over medium-high heat. Add the garlic and sauté until very lightly browned, about 2 1/2 minutes. Add the tomatoes and cook until the juices thicken, about 12 minutes. Season with salt and pepper.

3. Meanwhile, bring a large pot of salted water to a boil; reduce the heat to a gentle simmer, and cook the ravioli until tender, 5 to 8 minutes.

4. Drain the ravioli. Add to the pan, tossing with the tomato sauce. Stir in the pine nuts and basil. Taste and adjust the seasonings.

5. Serve immediately in bowls. Garnish with a big pinch of the grated cheese. Pass around a bowl of the leftover cheese at the table.

Serves 6

high-rollin' pasta

with lobster sauce

It happens to every guy at some time. You've got to move beyond the clam sauce and rethink your status as Mr. Can Opener. When the heavy hitters are on the guest list, you need a springboard on which to display your devastating charms and culinary savoir faire. For that client who could be your ticket to early retirement or for prospective in-laws unimpressed with your thrift-store tie, the following is all about looking good. The ingredients appear basic, but grab some freshly cooked lobster (or even big prawns) at the fish counter, and suddenly your star is rising. The recipe comes from the artistic kitchen of Victoria Frey, the Mark McGwire of dinner-party throwers.

- 1/2 cup olive oil
- 1/4 cup chopped shallots (about 2 medium) or yellow onions
- 1/4 cup finely chopped garlic (about 6 cloves)
- 1/3 cup dry white wine
- Juice of 2 lemons
- Salt and freshly ground pepper
- 1 pound long-strand pasta, such as bucatini or linguine
- 1 pound cooked lobster tail meat, cut diagonally into 1/2-inch-thick slices
- 1/4 cup chopped fresh flat-leaf (Italian) parsley
- 3 tablespoons grated Parmesan cheese

1. Warm the oil in a large skillet over medium heat. Add the shallots and garlic and sauté until translucent, about 3 minutes. Add the wine and lemon juice and cook a few minutes to blend. Season generously with salt and pepper.

2. Bring a large pot of salted water to a boil; cook the pasta until al dente, with resistance to the bite.

3. Meanwhile, add the lobster slices to the skillet and sauté until just pink outside and cooked inside, 6 to 8 minutes. Stir in the parsley.

4. Drain the pasta and add it to the skillet, tossing quickly to blend with the sauce. Taste and adjust the seasonings.

5. Transfer to a serving platter. Garnish with the cheese and serve hot.

Serves 4

peter's principled

This dish is so simple, it seems almost boastful to call it a recipe. If you want to score points with the powers over your paycheck, call it by its traditional name, *coscia 'i maiali arrustutu,* Sicilian for roast loin of pork. As interpreted by our food-hound friend Peter Sistrom, the dish should be served ideally at room temperature with a minimum of sauce. It's all about the flavor of caramelized, near-burnt onions that cling to the meat with a deep, sweet pungency. On the side? Something colorful, like mashed sweet potatoes or butternut squash, and a tart fruit, not to mention a bottle of robust wine.

pork tenderloin

- 1¹/₂ pounds boneless pork loin
- Salt and freshly ground pepper
- 1¹/₂ cups finely chopped yellow onions (about 3 small onions)
- 1 cup dry white wine

1. Preheat the oven to 500 degrees F.

2. Rinse the pork and pat dry. Generously salt and pepper both sides. Place on a rack fitted inside a roasting pan. Mound the onions over the top and sides. It's okay if pieces fall to the bottom of the pan, but make sure the surfaces are well coated.

3. Bake 15 minutes to sear and brown the onions. Open the oven door briefly and reduce the heat to 375 degrees F; bake 20 minutes.

4. Remove the pan from the oven. Carefully pour the wine over the onions, using a zigzag motion to evenly cover the surface. Be careful not to displace the onion crust. Return the pork to the oven. Cook 10 minutes for medium with a slightly pink center, which is ideal, or 15 minutes for well done.

5. Remove the pork from the oven. Slip a spatula underneath the tenderloin and transfer to a carving board. Remove the roasting rack. Scrape up as much of the crispy, caramelized onions as possible and sprinkle over the pork. Carve the meat into thin slices and serve warm or cool to room temperature.

Serves 6

jammin' dishwasher salmon

It's not an urban myth. You really *can* cook fish in a hot dishwasher, and no doubt it was a dude that first figured this out. When the fish is tightly wrapped in foil and run through the cycle (no, you don't use detergent), the process is actually a close cousin to steamed fish. So, why bother with the big clanker? Because it's fun. Your guests will marvel at your engineering skills and sense of humor. Gather for cocktails around the machine, and explain the concept to the tune of the sloshing. They won't believe how great it all turns out, especially with spoonfuls of mango salsa mingled with rum-soaked raisins.

- 2 pounds center-cut salmon fillet (no thicker than 1 1/4 inches)
- 1 orange, cut into 1/8-inch slices
- 4 tablespoons orange juice concentrate
- 1 teaspoon fresh or dried thyme
- Mango Mojo (page 84)

1. Rince the salmon fillet and pat dry. Remove any noticeable bones with a needle-nose pliers.

2. On a flat surface, pull out a length of aluminum foil long enough to cover and fold over the fish, plus a little extra. Place the orange slices in the middle and arrange the salmon on top. Spread the concentrate over the salmon, and sprinkle with the thyme. Bring the short ends of the foil together, meeting in the middle of the fish. Align the edges evenly and fold them over at least twice, crimping the final edge. Bring the long side edges together, folding and crimping in the same manner.

3. Place the bundle on the top rack of an empty dishwasher. Close the door and set the machine on a normal cycle. When the entire cycle is completed, remove the salmon — it should be moist and cooked through. If not, run back through the cycle another 5 to 7 minutes. Unwrap and transfer to a serving platter. Serve the Mango Mojo as a condiment on the side.

Serves 4

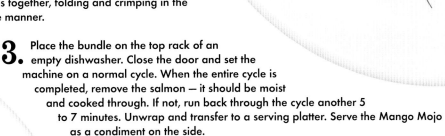

patio

chapter 4
daddy-o

Long before you were dealt a hot hand, before the thrill of hot wheels, even before your first hot date, there was the heat of barbecue. Let's face it: At heart, every guy's a pyromaniac — and the backyard pit is where you get away with it. What you can't get away with is wimpy recipes: Barbecue is the most performance intensive of a man's culinary rites, a signature of artful, soulful summer feasting. The following dishes will help ease the passage and turn a bachelor's bash into a triumph of the grill.

The Menu
- **Name That Tuna**
- **Bad-Boy Burgers**
- **Atomic Chicken**
- **Great Legs**
- **Bone-Gnawing, Brown-Sugared, Lip-Buzzing BBQ Ribs**

name that tuna

What's a barbecue without big rosy slabs of tuna, smoldering over hot coals? No other fish seems to take so well to smoke and fire and infusions of flavors that can go in just about any direction. This version conveys a healthy profile and a taste of Asian soul, with fillets steeped for several hours in a pool of soy, sesame, and cilantro. After a quick sizzle, expect sparks to rocket around your mouth. Lisa Shara Hall, the recipe's food-crazy creator, says this marinade also works wonders with flank steak, boneless chicken breasts, or other steaklike fish fillets. Off-season, you can cook the marinated goods in the oven, one inch below a hot broiler.

MARINADE
- Juice of 1 orange
- Juice of 3 limes or lemons
- 1 slice fresh ginger, about 1 inch thick
- 1 garlic clove, minced
- 3/4 cup fresh cilantro leaves
- 1/2 cup soy sauce
- 5 drops Tabasco sauce
- 3 tablespoons sesame oil
- Freshly ground pepper to taste

- Four 6-ounce tuna fillets, each about 1 inch thick
- 2 limes, quartered

1. Combine the marinade ingredients and pour into a large freezer bag. Add the tuna fillets and close the bag tightly. Marinate 3 to 4 hours at room temperature or refrigerated, but no longer, turning occasionally.

2. Prepare a charcoal fire; meanwhile drain off the marinade and discard.

3. When the coals are medium-hot, with a faint red glow and a thick coat of gray ash, grill the tuna until opaque on the outside and medium-rare in the center, 3 to 4 minutes on each side.

4. Serve with the quartered limes for a final flavor flourish.

Serves 4

bad-boy burgers

Burgers plumped with spicy sausage will turn pedestrian grub into patties of pure, sinful delight, especially when tucked between toasted buns slathered with garlic mayo (remember . . . happiness is a warm bun). Might as well go all the way and have a mountain of Sweet Potato Chips (page 79) and a monster slice of The Dude's Chocolate Cake (page 92).

BURGERS
- 1 3/4 pounds ground round steak
- 3/4 pound ground pork
- 1/2 pound andouille or other spicy sausage, cut into small pieces
- Freshly ground pepper to taste
- 1 teaspoon dried thyme
- 1/2 teaspoon dried oregano

GARLIC MAYO
- 1/4 cup mayonnaise
- 2 or 3 small garlic cloves, squeezed through a garlic press
- 1 tablespoon fresh lemon juice

- 6 split onion buns or kaiser rolls
- 6 red onion slices
- 6 tomato slices
- Leafy lettuce or mixed field greens

1. Combine all the burger ingredients in a mixing bowl. Cover and set aside.

2. Prepare a charcoal fire. Meanwhile, divide the burger mixture into 6 equal balls, flattening each so that it's about 1 inch thick.

3. Combine all the garlic mayonnaise ingredients, and season with freshly ground pepper.

4. When the coals are medium-hot, with a faint red glow and thick coat of ash, grill the burgers on the grill rack, 4 to 5 minutes on each side for medium, a little longer for well done.

5. Remove the burgers to a platter. Lightly toast the buns on the grill, cut side down. Serve the burgers on toasted buns with onions, tomatoes, lettuce, and garlic mayo on the side.

Serves 6

atomic chicken

Maybe it's the breast thing, but guys love to fire up that chicken, especially during the barbecue playoff season, running May through Labor Day. Marinades are a personality test, the place where you reveal whether you're a sweet, spicy, or wild kind of guy. The atomic bird is for the risk-taker, a dude willing to orbit above the predictable red barbecue sauce. Who else would blast a lemon-soaked marinade with the woody tones of bourbon, then seal the deal with a pop of orange-lime glaze? Just remember to get the marinade going the night before.

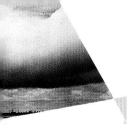

MARINADE
- •¹/₂ cup fresh lemon juice
- •¹/₂ cup brown sugar
- •3 garlic cloves, squeezed through a garlic press
- •¹/₄ cup bourbon, such as Jack Daniel's
- •Salt and freshly ground pepper

- •Two 3-pound chickens, quartered
- •³/₄ cup orange juice concentrate, thawed
- •2 teaspoons grated lime rind
- •¹/₄ cup fresh lime juice

1. The night before serving: Combine the marinade ingredients. Place the chicken in a large, shallow glass or enamel pan with the marinade, turning to coat each piece. Cover and refrigerate 8 hours or overnight, turning occasionally.

2. Prepare a charcoal fire. Meanwhile, bring the chicken to room temperature; drain off and discard the marinade.

3. Combine the orange juice concentrate and lime rind in a small bowl. Measure out ¹/₄ cup of the mixture, and set aside.

4. When the coals are hot, with a red glow and a thin layer of gray ash, grill the chicken, skin side down, turning occasionally and basting frequently with the orange-lime mixture. Cook until the skin is crisp and the juices run clear (not pink) when the meat is pierced, 8 to 12 minutes.

5. Transfer to a platter. Combine the fresh lime juice with the reserved orange-lime mixture; pour over the chicken to serve.

Serves 6

great legs

Sure, you were busy. Snooping around all those Web sights, mentionable and otherwise, is a full-time job. But what about those people you invited over — that's right, tonight. Even the most disorganized can pick up a leg of lamb, let it wallow in a marinade thirty to sixty minutes, then roast it to perfection over hot coals. But next time, plan ahead: Marinate the meat overnight and watch your barbecue creds soar even higher. The following game plan comes by way of our friend, food and wine writer Matt Kramer, who has mastered the art of cooking . . . and living.

- 1 cup olive oil
- 1/2 cup fresh lemon juice
- 4 garlic cloves, very thinly sliced
- 1/2 cup finely chopped flat-leaf (Italian) parsley
- 3 or 4 sprigs fresh thyme, rosemary, or oregano
- Salt and freshly ground pepper to taste
- One 6-pound leg of lamb, boned and butter-flied by the butcher

1. Whisk together all the ingredients except the lamb in a mixing bowl. Place the lamb in a large, deep glass or porcelain bowl or tray large enough to hold it completely. Pour on the marinade; using your hands, make sure that both sides of the lamb are coated.

2. Marinade 30 to 60 minutes at room temperature, turning occasionally. Or refrigerate overnight and let sit 1 or 2 hours at room temperature before cooking.

3. Prepare a charcoal fire. Drain the marinade from the lamb and reserve.

4. When the coals are hot, with a red glow and evenly coated with white ash, spread them in an even layer. Raise the grill 2 to 3 inches above the coals (depending upon heat intensity). Grill 15 minutes on one side, then turn and grill another 5 to 8 minutes, basting frequently with the reserved marinade. The lamb is medium-rare when rosy "pearls" form on the cooked side of the meat after it's been flipped. A finger pressed gently into the meat will have some give, yet also sense some resistance. Inevitably, the thicker parts of the butterflied lamb leg will be rarer than the thinner parts. (It's often easiest to start serving from the thinner parts first and return the thicker part to the grill to finish cooking, as needed.)

5. Place the lamb on a cutting board and let rest 10 minutes to allow the juices to recede into the meat. Then cut into thin slices.

Serves 8

bone-gnawing, brown-

The entire cult of barbecue is founded on a spiced slab of ribs. Period. There's something about the primal, meat-on-the-bone experience that brings out the raw appetite, the urge to hunch over something at once uncivilized and glorious. Your ribs résumé should include several different sauces that leave no doubt as to who is lord of the pit, including one shortcut version that transforms a bottled sauce into a smoky, expressionistic brew. The following does just that. We like Open Pit Barbecue Sauce as a base, but cut loose with your favorite sauce or heat source. For the tenderest ribs, ask the butcher to remove the tough membrane from the back side of the meat.

sugared, lip-buzzing bbq ribs

- •3 racks pork ribs, each 3 pounds
- •Ground black pepper to taste
- •Garlic powder to taste

SAUCE
- •One 28-ounce bottle barbecue sauce
- •Freshly ground pepper to taste
- •Garlic powder to taste
- •3 tablespoons fresh lemon juice
- •2 tablespoons brown sugar
- •2 tablespoons distilled white vinegar
- •4 to 6 ounces dark beer
- •2 teaspoons chili powder
- •1 teaspoon hot sauce
- •2 teaspoons liquid smoke

- •1 cup hickory chips (optional)

1. Sprinkle the ribs lightly on both sides with pepper and garlic powder.

2. To make the sauce: Combine the sauce ingredients in a 2-quart saucepan. Bring to a boil over medium heat, stirring occasionally. Remove from the heat, and set aside.

3. Prepare a charcoal fire. Soak the hickory chips in water to cover. When the coals are hot, push them to one side of the grill to create a source of "indirect heat." Drain the chips and sprinkle half of them over the coals. Place a disposable foil pan in the center of the bottom grate to catch drippings.

4. Grill the ribs on the part of the cooking rack without hot coals under it, turning occasionally. After 20 minutes, sprinkle the remaining chips over the coals. When the ribs are brown and almost done (around 50 minutes), slather the back (boney) side with the sauce, turning after 10 minutes. Then slather the front (meaty) side and cook until tender, 10 to 15 minutes. Serve with additional sauce on the side.

Serves 6

chapter 5

mr. mom

The kids have arrived for the weekend, and you need to figure out the three or four things they'll actually eat. Stick to the basics. Don't even consider anything with tofu. This fail-safe recipe collection includes magical peanut butter and chocolate sandwiches; tomato soup spaghetti; and crunchy-munchy, cheese-crusted chicken. Call on these creations when you want to keep small tongues happy and your illusions of control intact.

The Menu

- Peanut Butter Heaven
- Mama Bob's Baked Spaghetti
- Fake-Out Fried Chicken
- Shake It Up, Baby
- Heap of Cream Cheese Eggs
- Your Own Private Idahos

peanut butter heaven

You already know the power of squooshy bread chunked with peanut butter and sliced bananas. But spread on Nutella, a blissful chocolate-hazelnut spread, and you've gone beyond anything conceived by the grape jelly folks. This addition might get you in trouble with the sugar cops (also known as your "ex"), but be assured you'll score big points with the little crowd. You can always go to court and plead nutritional ignorance later. Nutella is available in many grocery stores, but you can substitute your favorite chocolate spread.

- 2 slices soft white sandwich bread
- 2 tablespoons peanut butter
- 2 tablespoons Nutella
- $1/2$ medium banana, cut into $1/4$-inch slices

1. Spread one slice of bread with peanut butter, the other slice with Nutella.

2. Place the banana slices on top of the Nutella and cover with the other peanut buttered slice. Cut in half and serve.

Serves 1

mama bob's baked spaghetti

With kids the rule is simple: The more orange the food, the more they like it. Here, Velveeta cheese, the ultimate color shock on a plate, is combined with tomatoey things and skinny spaghetti, then baked to all its gaudy glory. Sure, it's the essence of fifties retro-trash cooking, but there's no denying a special deliciousness — like eating tomato soup, grilled cheese, and spaghetti ragu all at once. Kids will relish it with more wild enthusiasm than anything you could assemble from an upscale deli.

- 12 ounces spaghettini
- One 10 3/4-ounce can tomato soup
- One 8-ounce can tomato sauce
- 12 ounces Velveeta cheese, cut into chunks
- 1 teaspoon salt
- 1/2 teaspoon ground black pepper

1. Preheat the oven to 350 degrees F.

2. Bring a large pot of salted water to a boil. Break the spaghettini into thirds and add to the boiling water. Cook until tender.

3. Meanwhile, mix the remaining ingredients together in a huge bowl.

4. Drain the spaghettini in a colander and combine with the tomato soup–cheese mixture. Place in an ungreased 2^1/2-quart casserole dish, cover, and bake 45 minutes.

5. Remove the lid. Continue baking until the top looks crusty, about 15 minutes. Serve hot.

Serves 6

fake-out fried chicken

Kids are notoriously down on eating chicken skin — it's the icky texture thing. On the other hand, they love just about anything fried. Here, you get the best of both worlds: skinless meat, butter-dipped and cheese-battered, then baked to a crispy, golden finish. It's an old trick from the New Jersey home of food writer Lisa Shara Hall, and still a child-pleaser today. You can buy prepackaged Parmesan shreds as an easy shortcut, but freshly grated cheese will make these babies soar.

- 4 skinless, boneless chicken breasts
- 2 cups buttermilk
- Butter or cooking spray
- 1/2 cup dried bread crumbs
- 1/2 cup grated Parmesan cheese
- Salt and ground black pepper
- 2 tablespoons butter, melted

1. Trim the chicken breasts of any fat, cartilage, or underside flaps. Sandwich the breasts between 2 squares of plastic wrap or waxed paper. Now, here's the fun part: Using a mallet or the bottom of a small heavy frying pan, pound the breasts to 1/4-inch thickness.

2. Pour the buttermilk into a large Ziploc bag or a glass baking dish large enough to hold the chicken. Soak the breasts in the buttermilk for 20 minutes (any additional time is not necessary, but won't hurt, either).

3. Preheat the oven to 375 degrees F. Rub a baking pan with butter or coat with cooking spray.

4. Mix the crumbs and cheese with a little salt and pepper on a large plate. Remove the chicken from the buttermilk, shaking off any excess. Toss the breasts in the crumb mixture, one at a time, pressing on the crumbs with your fingers.

5. Place the coated chicken pieces in the baking pan; drizzle the butter over the tops. Bake until crispy and deep golden brown, about 50 minutes.

Serves 4

shake it up, baby

Your teen portfolio must include a strong repertoire of milkshakes. We'll get you started with the basic chocolate/vanilla profile, and give you blueprints for building three taste variations. (Nothing complex here: peanut butter, bananas, orange juice.) If you're feeling guilty or right-eous, you can replace the ice cream with frozen yogurt. Or go in the other direction and indulge the obsessions of the moment, from crushed Oreos to crumbled Butterfinger candy bars.

- 1 cup (1/2 pint) vanilla or chocolate ice cream
- 1/2 cup milk
- 2 tablespoons chocolate syrup

1. Combine the ice cream, milk, and chocolate syrup in a blender. Mix at high speed until smooth. Pour into a tall, frosty glass.

Serves 1

VARIATIONS

Peanut Butter Blitz: Add 2 tablespoons creamy peanut butter. You can also add 1/2 small ripe banana. Eliminate the chocolate syrup to intensify the peanut butter flavor, or add up to 3 tablespoons of syrup for an ultra-rich combo.

Tangerine Dream: Omit the milk and substitute tangerine or orange juice (the fresher, the better).

Nutty Caramel: Add 1 tablespoon creamy peanut butter, 2 tablespoons caramel sauce, and a few shakes of ground cinnamon.

heap of cream cheese eggs

When all else fails, you can always fall back on the scrambled egg plan anytime of day. We offer two great secrets for the perfect batch. First, don't "scramble" the eggs by stirring furiously. Think of a slo-mo bulldozer just big enough to fit in the pan, methodically plowing across the field of eggs. The result is big, fluffy mounds of pure sunshine. Second, you need only one addition: cream cheese. The cubes melt in slightly, creating little pockets of richness.

- 8 large eggs
- 3 tablespoons milk
- 1 1/2 tablespoons butter
- 4 ounces cream cheese, at room temperature, cut into small cubes
- Salt and freshly ground black pepper

1. Crack the eggs into a medium mixing bowl. Add the milk and whisk briskly to blend, but don't overbeat.

2. Melt the butter in a large skillet over medium heat. After the butter has melted, and the foam begins to subside, add the egg mixture. You must work quickly at this point. Distribute the cream cheese cubes evenly over the top of the eggs. Then position a spatula, slant side down, at the end of the skillet closest to you. Push the spatula away from you and across the pan, plowing the cooked eggs along the bottom as you go. With every push across the pan, portions of cooked eggs will pile up at one end, like snowdrifts.

3. Continue cooking until all the eggs are just barely firm, fluffy, and moist. Season with salt and pepper to serve.

Serves 4

your own private idahos

A baked potato is not exactly a twelve-year-old's thrill treat, but with a little engineering on the inside, you can transform this one-trick pony into a carousel of flavors. Crumbles of sausage, a smear of sour cream, and a handful of fragrant herbs will get you off to a good start. Let your imagination roam, and create your own universe inside that humble skin.

- 4 large Idaho or russet potatoes
- 1/2 to 3/4 pound ground sausage meat
- 1/4 cup finely chopped fresh flat-leaf (Italian) parsley leaves
- 1/4 cup finely chopped fresh basil leaves, or 1 tablespoon dried
- 2 garlic cloves, finely chopped
- 1 large egg, slightly beaten
- Salt and freshly ground pepper
- Sour cream or extra-virgin olive oil for garnish

1. Preheat the oven to 425 degrees F.

2. Scrub the potatoes well and prick several times with a fork. Bake until tender, about 1 hour. Remove from the oven.

3. Meanwhile, in a large skillet over medium heat, sauté the sausage until lightly browned and cooked through, 5 to 7 minutes. Stir in the parsley, basil, and garlic. Stir in the egg. Sauté until the mixture clumps slightly and the egg is cooked, about 2 minutes. Remove from the heat.

4. Cut the potatoes lengthwise into two halves, and scoop the "meat" from the skins with a spoon. Cool briefly. Combine the potato meat with the sausage mixture, and season with salt and pepper. Stuff each potato half with this filling. Serve lukewarm or reheat in the oven. Garnish with sour cream or drizzle a little olive oil over each half.

Serves 4

VARIATION: Substitute 2 to 3 tablespoons pesto for the parsley and basil.

the lone

chapter 6
ranger

When there's no one around to cook for but your lonesome, take our advice: Do not eat over the sink. At these times, there's no comfort like comfort foods, things warm and soul-satisfying to take over to the couch on a date with the VCR. Eggs souped up with smoky barbecue sauce, deluxe oatmeal glorified in apple juice, and colorful bean soup from the fast lane — these are fixings to outfit the chuck wagon when you're in the saddle alone.

THE MENU

- **Texas Smokehouse Eggs**
- **Soup Dreams**
- **Rock-a-Billy's Cowboy Chicken**
- **Only the Lonely Ravioli**
- **Cereal Monogamy**

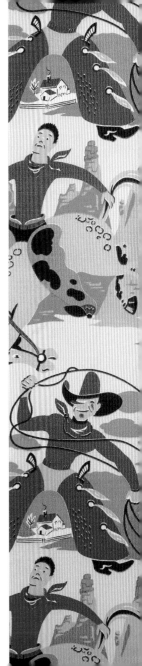

texas smokehouse

Whip up a few eggs with a bold splash of mesquite-scented barbecue sauce and a fistful of cheese, then scramble away. With its heady bonfire perfume, this dish works just as well at sundown as at sunrise. Side with meaty avocado slices, and hitch up some buttered garlic toast or a grilled flour tortilla. Horse around with some other breeds, too, from spicy green tomatillo salsa instead of the sauce, to aged cheddar instead of Gouda.

eggs

- •3 large eggs
- •3 tablespoons milk
- •1 1/2 tablespoons mesquite-flavored barbecue sauce, such as Texas Barbeque Sauce
- •1 cup grated smoked Gouda cheese
- •1 teaspoon butter
- •1/2 avocado, sliced

1. Crack the eggs into a mixing bowl. Whisk in the milk and 1 tablespoon of the barbecue sauce. Blend well but don't overbeat. Whisk in the cheese.

2. Heat the butter in a small skillet over medium heat. When the butter has melted and the foam begins to subside, add the egg mixture. As soon as the eggs start to firm (about 10 seconds), position a spatula, slanted side down, at the end of the skillet closest to you. Push the spatula away from you and across the pan, plowing portions of cooked eggs along the bottom as you go. When finished, the eggs will be piled up at one end, like snowdrifts.

3. Cook until all the eggs are just barely firm, fluffy, and moist.

4. Transfer to a plate. Spread the remaining 1/2 tablespoon of barbecue sauce over the top and surround with avocado slices.

Serves 1

soup dreams

Here's the perfect Sunday night score: a colorful, carbo-charged soup that comes together with the speed of a fast break. Whip up a piquant pot, and you've got nothin' but net. Store leftovers in the fridge for quick midweek dinners. The game plan comes courtesy of all-star soup man George Eltman.

- One 14^1/$_2$-ounce can vegetable broth
- 3^1/$_2$ cups water
- One 19-ounce can black beans, drained
- One 15-ounce can white beans, drained
- 1 large red bell pepper, seeded and chopped
- 1 cup frozen corn kernels
- Juice of 2 lemons
- 1 cup fresh cilantro leaves
- Salt and freshly ground pepper to taste
- Favorite hot sauce to taste

1. In a soup pot or a large saucepan, combine the broth, water, beans, red pepper, corn, and lemon juice. Cook 25 minutes over medium heat, stirring occasionally. Reduce the heat to simmer. Add the cilantro leaves. Season with salt, pepper, and hot sauce.

2. Cook until the flavors are blended and the red peppers are tender, about 5 more minutes. Taste and adjust the seasonings. Serve hot.

Makes 2 quarts

rock-a-billy's

What do you get when you toss a butter-and-vermouth-washed bird into a furnace hot enough to melt a branding iron? A bronzed beauty shot through with brushfire flavors fanned by lemon and herbs. Flavor desperado Billy Galperin, who wrangled the original idea, recommends using a kosher or free-range chicken for superior taste and texture. You can chow down on this all week, using leftovers in sandwiches and salads.

cowboy chicken

- One 3 1/2- to 4-pound chicken, ideally kosher or free-range
- 1 lemon, quartered
- 1 bunch of fresh thyme, or 2 tablespoons dried
- 6 garlic cloves
- 1 tablespoon ground pepper

BASTING SAUCE
- 1 tablespoon butter
- 1/2 cup vermouth

1. Preheat the oven to 500 degrees F.

2. Wash the chicken and pat dry. Discard the giblets. Squeeze the lemon quarters inside the chicken cavity. Place 2 of the quarters in the very back of the cavity, followed by the thyme. Lay the garlic cloves on top of the thyme, sprinkle with pepper, and add the remaining lemon quarters.

3. Place the chicken on its back in a roasting pan. Melt the butter in a saucepan. Remove from the heat, and stir in the vermouth. Drizzle half the mixture over the chicken. Bake 20 minutes.

4. Remove the chicken from the oven. Using a flat spatula and a carving fork, turn the chicken over onto its breast. Return to the oven for 20 minutes.

5. Remove the chicken from the oven and turn it over, breast side up. Drizzle the remaining basting sauce on top. Roast until dark golden brown all over, about 20 minutes.

6. Remove the chicken from the pan and transfer to a carving board. Let rest 10 minutes before slicing.

Serves 4 (or 1 person, 4 times)

only the lonely ravioli

A brave new world of ravioli exists in hipster markets and pasta shops. Scout out a flavor as a foundation, then build it into something fun and original. A Piedmontese sauce of melted butter mingled with nothing but the bright pungency of fresh sage will elevate just about any species into an instant party for one. The proportions can easily be multiplied should unexpected company arrive.

- •9 ounces ravioli
- •2 tablespoons unsalted butter
- •2 large fresh sage leaves, very finely chopped
- •2 to 3 tablespoons freshly grated Parmesan cheese

1. Bring a large pot of salted water to a boil; reduce the heat to a gentle simmer and cook the ravioli until tender.

2. Meanwhile, melt the butter in a small saucepan over low heat. Add the sage and remove from the heat. The longer the mixture sits, the better the flavor. You can remelt the butter before serving, if necessary.

3. Drain the ravioli. Toss with the melted butter mixture and top with Parmesan cheese.

Makes 1 serving

VARIATION: Replace the butter with olive oil and a good pinch of dried red pepper flakes. When the oil is hot, add 1 sliced garlic clove and sauté.

oat cuisine

cereal monogamy

Sure, you can dump a box of dry flakes in a bowl and slurp it down with milk. But how about an alternative, something compelling enough to lure you away from the newspaper to spend a few minutes over the stove. How about oatmeal sublime enough to warrant a serious commitment? What will grab your attention is this: oats, fresh fruit, raisins, and sweet spices cooked in apple juice until they marry up into a hot flavor rush. Pile on our stash of extras, such as crushed walnuts and cream, for the ultimate experience.

- 1 1/4 cups apple juice
- 1/2 cup water
- 1 cup rolled oats, such as Quaker's Old-Fashioned Oats
- 1 small ripe banana, sliced, or 1/2 pear, peeled and chopped
- 1/4 cup raisins
- Big pinch each: cinnamon and nutmeg
- 1 generous teaspoon butter

TOPPINGS (any or all)
- Maple syrup
- Half-and-half or milk
- A few crushed walnuts
- 1 teaspoon butter

1. Bring the apple juice and water to a boil in a medium saucepan. Stir in the oats and banana slices or pear chunks. Reduce the heat to medium and cook 2 minutes, stirring occasionally.

2. Stir in the raisins, cinnamon, nutmeg, and butter. Cook until the liquid evaporates and the oatmeal is thick and a little sticky, stirring constantly 3 to 5 minutes.

3. Transfer to a bowl and add any of the desired toppings.

Serves 1 generously

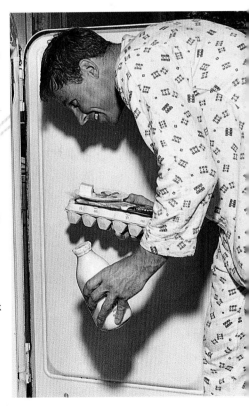

side

chapter 7
kicks

Think of these dishes as accessories, things that require a little skill in matching with an entrée, like finding the tie that works best with a plaid shirt — no, not the paisley tie. The following dishes should complement both serious and quirky cooking. From dinner parties to patio bashes to candlelit affairs, your options to mix and match are high. Remember, spicy sides go best with mellow main courses and vice versa. Choose things that bring different colors to the meal, and you'll be a regular fashion plate.

The Menu
- **Monster Mash**
- **Sweet Potato Chips**
- **The Ultimate Caesar**
- **Burning Spears**
- **Lord of the Fries**
- **Shroom Service**
- **Mango Mojo**
- **Macho Ball Soup**

monster mash

The hell with comfort food. This is killer food. Simple. Substantial. Packs a sharp punch. Mom's whipped mashed potatoes — and, God knows, those mannered roasted garlic mashed potatoes — are ghostly in the face of hand-wrecked spuds seasoned with imported Italian Romano cheese and cracked pepper. The trick? Doing the very least to achieve rough texture and bursting flavor by using muscle and only a few very fine ingredients. Be prepared for your guests to ask: What is this stuff? You won't tell them: Salty sheep cheese warring with pungent pepper while a great potato wave engulfs and blunts, leaving a haunting flavor that is both earthy and ethereal. You might, however, tell them: Hey, a man has to make a choice in life, to ski the mountain sensibly in stretch pants or bomb it in trusty old jeans. By meal's end, says Monster creator Len Reed, they'll understand — and ask for seconds.

- 4 medium-large russet baking potatoes
- Freshly ground pepper
- 1 cup whole milk, at room temperature
- 1 cup (4 ounces) freshly grated Romano cheese, preferably imported Locatelli Pecorino

1. Preheat the oven to 350 degrees F.

2. Scrub the potatoes well and prick several times with a fork. Bake the potatoes until fork-tender, 45 to 60 minutes.

3. Quickly slit the potatoes lengthwise, lay open, and scoop out the meat from the skins with a spoon. Discard the skins. The key is to work fast enough to keep the potatoes hot. Place the potatoes in a large mixing bowl and generously grind the pepper over the top, at least 10 full twists of the pepper mill. Stir in 1/2 cup milk and 3/4 cup of the cheese.

4. Mash away, using a spoon from time to time to bring thick pieces into the center. Be sure the cheese melts and ingredients are blended, but don't overmash; you want lumps.

5. Taste and adjust the flavors. Too thick and dry? Mash in more of the milk. Not enough punch? Add more cheese and pepper.

Serves 4 to 6

soul mate
sweet potato chips

Homemade potato chips have great rhythm and none of the blues that come with the packaged species. These thin baked rounds, sprinkled with brown sugar and freshly grated nutmeg, hit you like funky soul music: Each bite is a jumping, sweet sensation. These are great couch potatoes, but also perfect for barbecues and steaks. Ketchup would be a crime, but if you must dunk, chunky applesauce will do the trick.

- 4 medium sweet potatoes
- 6 tablespoons unsalted butter
- Brown sugar to taste
- Salt to taste
- Freshly grated nutmeg to taste

1. Preheat the oven to 400 degrees F. Line 2 baking sheets with aluminum foil.

2. Slice the potatoes crosswise into thin rounds.

3. Melt the butter in a saucepan, then pour it into a shallow dish. Dip both sides of each potato slice in the butter, then arrange the slices in a single layer on the baking sheets.

4. Bake until crisp and golden brown, 30 to 40 minutes; reverse the pans from front to back after 15 minutes to ensure even baking.

5. Remove from the oven and quickly drain on paper towels. Immediately sprinkle the chips lightly with brown sugar and salt, then grate a little fresh nutmeg over the tops. Serve warm.

Serves 6

the ultimate caesar

For most guys, only one salad really counts, a Caesar. There's nothing subtle about crunchy lettuce, pungent dressing, and flinty cheese. It's raw and powerful, the hard body of salads. But too many versions wimp out on flavor. What puts this one on top of the empire is its refusal to stint on the potency issues — garlic and anchovy. And instead of predictable torn lettuce leaves, it uses ultra-crisp hearts of romaine piled up like canoes and dispatched in true guy fashion: with your fingers. We went straight to the kitchen that conquered the legendary Caesar: Zefiro, an outpost of hip feeding in Portland, Oregon, where it remains the celebrated signature of the house.

DRESSING

- 1 egg, coddled (see Note, below)
- 1 heaping tablespoon minced garlic
- 2 teaspoons anchovy paste
- $1/2$ teaspoon salt
- 2 tablespoons fresh lemon juice
- $1/2$ cup good-quality olive oil
- $1/4$ cup freshly grated Parmesan cheese, preferably Parmigiano-Reggiano cheese

- 3 heads romaine lettuce, well chilled
- $1 1/2$ cups homemade or commercially prepared large croutons
- Freshly grated Parmigiano-Reggiano cheese for garnish
- Freshly ground pepper

1. To make the dressing: Peel the coddled egg. Whisk together the garlic, anchovy, salt, and lemon juice in a mixing bowl. Add the egg, whisking until thick, about 1 minute. Slowly drizzle in the oil, whisking vigorously to thicken. Whisk in the $1/4$ cup Parmigiano-Reggiano cheese. Taste and adjust the flavor.

2. Separate the romaine leaves, discarding the coarse outer leaves and saving the inner leaves and hearts.

3. Pour $1/2$ cup of the dressing in the bottom of an oversized mixing bowl. Add the croutons, tossing them in

burning spears

There's something about asparagus that classes up any meal. Forget all those complicated rituals about peeling, standing upright, and steaming. Instead, just rub with olive oil and coarse salt, then pop the spears in a super-hot oven until beautifully singed. Simple perfection.

- •1 pound medium asparagus
- •Olive oil to taste
- •Kosher salt to taste

1. Preheat the oven to 500 degrees F; adjust the rack to the upper shelf.

2. Wash the asparagus spears, snap off the tough stem ends, and dry completely with paper towels.

3. Place the asparagus on a baking sheet in a single layer. Drizzle the olive oil over the tops, and sprinkle lightly with salt. Roast until cooked through and nicely charred, about 10 minutes. Serve immediately.

Serves 4

the dressing until coated. Add the inner romaine leaves and hearts, tossing until coated.

4. Transfer to a salad bowl. Garnish generously with Parmigiano-Reggiano and freshly ground pepper, and serve.

Serves 6

NOTE: A traditional Caesar dressing uses raw egg. Because of the possibility of salmonella, this one uses a coddled egg to destroy harmful bacteria. Rinse the egg in warm water, then set it in a mug. Cover with boiling water, and let stand 1 minute. Immediately run cold water into the mug until the egg can be easily handled.

lord of the fries

Without fanfare, turn the lights down, seat your guests, pour the microbrews, and set out the main dish. Then bring on the fireworks: crispy, amber-toned potatoes to be flamed in Cognac. Torch these babies at the table, and wow the crowd with their smoky, brandied afterglow. These home fries flambé go perfectly with omelets, roast chicken, grilled fish, or just about any slice of beef.

- 1¹/2 pounds russet potatoes
- 2 tablespoons olive oil
- 3 tablespoons butter
- 2 tablespoons sliced shallots
- ¹/2 teaspoon salt
- ¹/2 teaspoon freshly ground pepper
- ¹/2 teaspoon chopped garlic
- ¹/4 cup Cognac

1. Preheat oven to 425 degrees F.

2. Cut the potatoes lengthwise into quarters, then slice each wedge into ¹/8-inch triangles.

3. Bring 2 quarts of water to a boil in a saucepan. Add the potatoes and boil 4 minutes to partially cook. Drain well in a colander, but do not rinse.

4. Place a large ovenproof serving dish in the oven.

5. Heat the oil and butter in a large skillet over medium heat. When the butter melts, add the shallots and cook 2 minutes. Raise the heat to medium-high, and add the potatoes, salt, and pepper. Sauté 8 minutes, stirring occasionally. Add the garlic and cook until the potatoes turn golden, 2 to 4 minutes.

6. Increase the heat to high. Cook until the potatoes turn crispy, about 2 minutes. Remove the hot serving dish from the oven and add the potatoes. Bring the dish to the table. Immediately pour the Cognac evenly over the potatoes and carefully ignite. When the alcohol burns away, the potatoes are ready to eat.

Serves 6

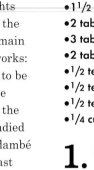
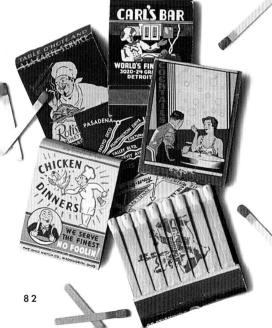

shroom service

Mushrooms are the perfect guy vegetable: easy to find and impossible to ruin, no matter how hard you try. Plus, they go with everything. These succulent little shrooms from pop culture scholar Lena Lencek will drive everyone back for seconds. Serve as a side dish or an uptown hors d'oeuvre alongside a nice bottle of red.

- 1 pound small whole mush-rooms or baby portobellos
- 3 tablespoons olive oil
- 4 garlic cloves, coarsely chopped
- 2 tablespoons minced flat-leaf (Italian) parsley leaves, plus a few sprigs for garnishing
- $1/2$ teaspoon juniper berries (optional)
- $1/4$ cup balsamic vinegar
- Juice of $1/2$ small lemon
- 1 teaspoon salt
- Freshly ground pepper

1. Trim away the mushroom stems and gently wipe the caps clean with paper towels (washing mushrooms ruins their flavor).

2. Heat the oil in a large skillet. Sauté the garlic over low heat until soft, about 5 minutes. Be careful not to burn. Add the mushrooms. Sauté over medium heat until they begin to color and the pan juices are bubbling. Add the parsley, juniper berries, and balsamic vinegar. Simmer about 10 minutes, flipping the mushrooms occasionally.

3. Season with the lemon juice, salt, and pepper. Remove from the heat. Serve warm as a side dish, garnished with parsley sprigs. Or cool and arrange on leafy lettuce as an appetizer.

Serves 4

mango mojo

Mojo means table sauce in Cuba, but in other Latin cultures the word is used to conjure the magical and the mystical. This is the best of both worlds, a table condiment that will cast a colorful flavor spell over grilled or poached fish, barbecued chicken, crab cakes, tortilla chips, or anything conjured up to fit inside a tortilla. With its rum-soaked raisins and ginger sting, this tropical fruit salsa from our friend Chris Hubert is guaranteed to turn a simple dish into a reggae afternoon.

- •¹/₂ cup rum
- •¹/₂ cup raisins
- •4 large, ripe mangos
- •2 tablespoons unsalted butter
- •1 small Vidalia or other sweet onion, finely chopped
- •1 small fresh red chile pepper, seeded and finely chopped (optional)
- •1 small green chile pepper, seeded and finely chopped
- •3 tablespoons grated fresh ginger
- •¹/₃ cup fresh lime juice
- •Salt to taste

1. Heat the rum in a small saucepan. Remove from the heat, add the raisins, and let stand 1 hour. Meanwhile, peel, core, and slice the mangos.

2. Melt the butter in a skillet over medium heat. Add the onion and sauté until translucent, about 3 minutes. Add the mango, chopped chile peppers, and ginger. Drain the raisins and discard the rum. Add the raisins to the skillet. Cook about 10 minutes to soften the fruit and chiles, and reduce the liquid, stirring. Remove from the heat. Stir in the lime juice, and season with salt.

Serves 6 to 8

macho ball soup

Aromas and childhood flavors can evoke serious sensations. They stimulate the neuronal jungle and open up one part of the brain to another, unleashing thoughts previously hidden beneath the threshold of consciousness. Which is why Freud would have appreciated this twisted take on your mother's matzo ball soup. We don't even want to consider the underlying message here, but we did consider the flavor: brazen. No doubt these bold dumplings will add some spice to a Friday night dinner conversation.

- 4 large eggs
- 1/2 cup kosher white extra-hot horse-radish
- 1/2 teaspoon minced garlic
- One box (2 packages) matzo ball mix, such as Streits Matzo Ball Mix
- 1/8 teaspoon white pepper
- 1/2 teaspoon baking powder
- 2 teaspoons salt
- 2 quarts best-quality low-salt canned chicken soup

1. With a fork, gently combine the eggs, horseradish, and garlic in a large mixing bowl.

2. Pour the matzo ball mix into a medium bowl. Stir in the pepper and baking powder. Add the mix to the egg mixture and blend thoroughly, but do not overbeat. Cover and let stand 15 minutes.

3. Meanwhile, bring a large pot of salted water to a boil; reduce the heat to a gentle simmer.

4. Run your hands under cold water. With moist hands, pinch off golf-ball-size portions of the matzo ball mixture and drop them into the simmering water. Cover and cook about 15 minutes, or until tender. Remove one matzo ball and cut in half to test for doneness.

5. Meanwhile, heat the chicken soup in a large saucepan or a soup pot. Add the matzo balls. Serve in bowls, allowing 2 or 3 balls per eater.

Makes 12 matzo balls; serves 4 to 6

sweet

chapter 8
talkin' guy

Treats off the shelf will tide you over in tough times, but face it: There's only so much fun in a cellophaned goodie stamped out by a factory on the other side of the planet. Fear of baking may be deep in your DNA, but these classics and creations for the debonair dessert hound are handpicked to minimize technique and maximize satisfaction. For late-night hankerings to party flavors to cooking with kids, these concoctions will leave everyone talking . . . with their mouths full.

THE MENU

- Beastie Bars
- Princely Pears in Port
- Electric Love Lounge Chocolate Chip Cookies
- Flame Boy Baked Alaska
- The Dude's Chocolate Cake

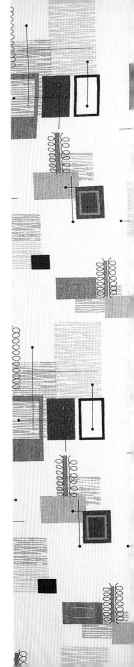

beastie bars

Most guys are closet sweet tooths. When you want to indulge, you don't want the whole neighborhood to know. It's gotta be fast, simple, and downright decadent. These unconscionably rich squares of badness are the ticket: part brownie, part candy bar, all heaven. If you want to go public, they will fit just about any occasion — take them to the beach or the office, to barbecues or family affairs. Experiment away with your own additions: Replace the grahams with gingersnaps, shortbread cookies, or even crushed Oreos. Select your chips of choice: peanut butter, butterscotch, or espresso. Get loose with that tooth . . . and be shameless.

- 4 whole graham crackers
- 4 tablespoons butter, melted
- 1/2 cup sweetened shredded coconut
- 1/2 cup semisweet chocolate chips
- 1/2 cup white chocolate chips
- 3/4 cup sweetened condensed milk
- One 4-ounce bag pecan bits
- Ground cinnamon to taste

1. Preheat oven to 350 degrees F.

2. In a blender or food processor, reduce the graham crackers to crumbs. Measure out 1 cup; discard the rest.

3. Combine the crumbs and melted butter, and press into the bottom of an 8-x-8-inch-square baking pan. Sprinkle the coconut evenly over the crust. Add a layer of semisweet chocolate chips and a layer of white chocolate chips. Pour the condensed milk evenly over the chips. Top with the pecan bits, gently pressing them halfway into the condensed milk. Sprinkle a little cinnamon on top.

4. Bake 25 to 30 minutes, or until the condensed milk sets. Cool completely. Cut into small squares to serve.

Serves 12

princely pears in port

Juicy poached pears heady with the warmth of a port glaze says "This guy knows how to be sweet" (fooled them, again). After a rich meal — perhaps a holiday extravaganza — this artful dessert is guaranteed to make you the prince of the party. A little dab of vanilla ice cream or sweet Italian mascarpone cheese on the side would be a noble gesture.

- •2 lemons, washed
- •6 firm but ripe Anjou pears, stems attached
- •2 cups port
- •1/2 teaspoon whole cloves
- •2 cinnamon sticks
- •1/2 cup brown sugar

1. With a hand grater or special "zesting tool," carefully grate the "zest" or rind (the thin, colored yellow part only; the white pith below is bitter) from the lemons. Set aside.

2. Level off the bottoms of the pears. Place upright in a large pot with the port, cloves, cinnamon sticks, and half of the reserved lemon zest. Cover the pot. Simmer over medium-low heat (the liquid should be barely bubbling) until tender, about 1 hour. Check occasionally to make sure all the liquid does not boil away; add a little port or water if necessary.

3. Sprinkle the brown sugar over the pears and liquid, and stir to combine. Bring the mixture to a boil over medium-high heat. Cook about 10 minutes to slightly reduce the sauce. Spoon a little sauce over each pear, then transfer to a serving platter.

4. Bring the remaining liquid to a rapid boil for 3 to 5 minutes, or until it looks like light syrup. Pour a little syrup over each pear. Garnish with the remaining lemon zest and serve.

Serves 6

electric love lounge chocolate chip cookies

If you only master one chocolate chip cookie recipe in your life, this is it: golden mounds chunked with walnuts and sparked by the nutlike richness of malted milk. Beneath it all, the pulse of ground espresso. This is mood food at its finest. Share a batch with your other — lights low, plenty of cushions on the couch, then lay back and get buzzed on love.

- 1 cup all-purpose flour
- 2 tablespoons malted milk powder
- 2 tablespoons instant espresso powder
- 8 tablespoons unsalted butter, softened at room temperature
- 1/3 cup white sugar
- 1/3 cup firmly packed brown sugar
- 1/8 teaspoon salt
- 1/2 teaspoon vanilla extract
- 1 large egg
- 1/2 teaspoon baking soda
- 1/2 teaspoon water
- 1 cup semisweet chocolate chips
- 1 cup chopped walnuts

1. Preheat the oven to 350 degrees F.

2. In a small bowl, combine the flour, malted milk powder, and espresso. In the bowl of an electric mixer (or in a large mixing bowl, using hand-held electric beaters or a wooden spoon), beat the butter until just barely creamy. Beat in the sugars until smooth. Blend in, one at a time, the salt, vanilla, egg, and flour mixture.

3. Dissolve the baking soda in the water, and blend into the batter. Stir in the chips and nuts by hand.

4. Line a cookie sheet with aluminum foil, shiny side up. For each cookie, measure out 1 tablespoon of batter and gently push it out onto the cookie sheet, round side up. Place the mounds 2 inches apart, about 12 to a sheet.

5. Bake 11 minutes, or until the cookies are just browned and barely spring back when gently pressed in the middle. Cool about 5 minutes on the foil before removing. Repeat the process with the remaining batter.

Makes about 3 1/2 dozen cookies

flame boy baked alaska

Baked Alaska is a classic — weird and wonderful. Born in the 1800s, celebrated in the Ozzie and Harriet fifties, and resurrected for the millennium, this impossible marriage of cake, ice cream, and a blazing hot oven happily defies all the laws of thermo-dynamics. Chemistry class was never this fun. Our friend Hugh Van Dusen has made this dinner party show-piece a quick study. Grab a Sara Lee pound cake, your favorite ice cream, a couple of eggs, and some candied citron (hailstones of chewy citrus found in the baking section). The fun part is torching the whole production with brandy.

- 1 pound cake
- 1/2 cup candied citron (optional)
- 1/2 pint best-quality coffee (or favorite flavor) ice cream
- 4 large eggs, at room temperature
- 2 tablespoons superfine sugar
- 1/2 cup brandy

1. Four hours before serving: Slice a layer of pound cake the entire length of the cake and 1 1/2 inches thick. Save the remaining cake for another use. With aluminum foil, wrap a small board or a double layer of cardboard slightly larger than the cake layer. If using the citron, sprinkle it evenly over the top of the cake. Remove the ice cream from the container, and cut it into thin rounds or squares. Make an even layer of ice cream slices over the cake. Cover the cake and board with plastic wrap and freeze.

2. Two hours before serving: Crack the eggs gently, one at a time, on the edge of a clean, dry bowl. Jostle the insides back and forth between the shells, letting only the egg whites fall into the bowl. Discard the yolks. With an electric mixer or wire whisk, whip the egg whites until soft peaks form. Add the sugar and whip until the meringue is thick and glossy, with firm peaks.

3. Remove the cake from the freezer; discard the plastic wrap. Gently spread the meringue over the top and sides of the ice cream and cake. Return the cake and board to the freezer, unwrapped.

4. When ready to serve: Preheat the oven to 500 degrees F. Put the cake and board in the oven. Bake until the meringue tips are browned, about 4 minutes. Be careful not to burn.

5. Gently warm the brandy in a small saucepan. Remove the cake and board from the oven and transfer the cake to a serving plate. Pour the brandy over the top and carefully ignite. When the flame dies out, cut into slices and serve immediately.

Serves 4

the dude's chocolate

OK, you've cruised through this entire book, pretending you don't mind serving trays, touches of elegance, and all the other artifacts of civilized eating. Time to be the guy you really are: scarfin' it down before it hits the table, straight out of the fridge at 2 A.M., and by the handful for breakfast. Is there any other way to eat chocolate cake? This one is tailor-made for a solo cruise or for sharing with best buds: dark, moist cake packed with soft chocolate chunks served right out of the skillet with a meltdown of Hershey bars as the secret frosting. Totally dudesville.

cake

- •$^1/_2$ cup unsweetened cocoa
- •$^1/_2$ cup cold water
- •1$^1/_2$ cups all-purpose flour
- •$^3/_4$ cup firmly packed brown sugar
- •$^1/_2$ cup white sugar
- •$^1/_2$ teaspoon salt
- •1 teaspoon baking soda
- •8 tablespoons unsalted butter, softened at room temperature
- •3 large eggs
- •$^1/_2$ cup buttermilk
- •1 tablespoon vanilla extract
- •Ten 1.55-ounce milk or dark chocolate bars, such as Hershey

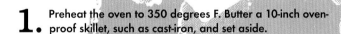

1. Preheat the oven to 350 degrees F. Butter a 10-inch oven-proof skillet, such as cast-iron, and set aside.

2. Blend the cocoa and water; set aside. In the bowl of an electric mixer (or in a large mixing bowl, using handheld beaters or just a wooden spoon) combine the flour, sugars, salt, and baking soda. Beat in the soft butter. The batter will look granular. On low speed, add the eggs and $^1/_4$ cup of the buttermilk. Beat at high speed until smooth, about 3 minutes, scraping down the sides with a rubber spatula. Blend in the vanilla, remaining buttermilk, and cocoa mixture at medium speed, about 2 minutes.

3. Pour the batter into the skillet. Break the chocolate bars into sections, placing half the pieces evenly over the top. Cover with a tight-fitting lid or aluminum foil. Bake 40 to 45 minutes, or until a toothpick inserted in the center of the cake comes out still moist but not wet.

4. Remove the cake from the oven. Distribute the remaining chocolate pieces over the top. Return to the oven, uncovered, until the chocolate is completely melted, 3 to 5 minutes. Remove from the oven. Smooth the melted chocolate with a table knife so that it resembles frosting. Serve immediately, right out of the skillet, at the table.

Serves 8

cooking terms

BASTE: Brushing or pouring liquid over food during the cooking process to encourage moistness and flavor. Use a special pastry brush, a basting bulb, or a spoon.

CARAMELIZE: Heating sugar and butter together until they thicken and acquire a rich caramel color and flavor.

GARNISH: To decorate food with something that adds color or flavor.

MARINATE: Letting meat, fish, fowl, or vegetables sit in a seasoned liquid to tenderize the food and add flavor.

MINCE: Very finely chopped

PUREE: To reduce food to a thick, smooth blend, usually in a blender or food processor.

SAUTÉ: Frequently stirring food in a hot skillet with a small amount of butter or oil until partially or completely cooked.

SEAR: To cook quickly over high heat to seal in juices and brown the surface.

SIMMER: Bringing liquid to a barely bubbling point over low heat.

WHISK: To whip in a brisk circular motion with a special wire whisk or a fork.

table of equivalents

The exact equivalents in the following tables have been rounded for convenience.

OVEN TEMPERATURE

Fahrenheit	Celsius	Gas
250	120	1/2
275	140	1
300	150	2
325	160	3
350	180	4
375	190	5
400	200	6
425	220	7
450	230	8
475	240	9
500	260	10

LENGTH

U.S.	Metric
1/8 inch	3 millimeters
1/4 inch	6 millimeters
1/2 inch	12 millimeters
1 inch	2.5 centimeters

LIQUID/DRY MEASURES

U.S.	Metric
1/4 teaspoon	1.25 milliliters
1/2 teaspoon	2.5 milliliters
1 teaspoon	5 milliliters
1 tablespoon (3 teaspoons)	15 milliliters
1 fluid ounce (2 tablespoons)	30 milliliters
1/4 cup	60 milliliters
1/3 cup	80 milliliters
1/2 cup	120 milliliters
1 cup	240 milliliters
1 pint (2 cups)	480 milliliters
1 quart (4 cups, 32 ounces)	960 milliliters
1 gallon (4 quarts)	3.84 liters
1 ounce (by weight)	28 grams
1 pound	454 grams
2.2 pounds	1 kilogram

index

acknowledgments

Breaking the code to a guy's culinary psyche required endless philosophical discussions, from the merits of eating over the sink to the meaning of a man and his steak. This involved chewing our way through strange and wonderful experiments and savvy insights from friends and family. And it required the kind of team work and commitment to quality that Chronicle Books has honed to an art form. For this, we thank our illustrious editor Bill LeBlond, his assistant Stephanie Rosenbaum, and our sharp-eyed copy editor, Deborah Kops.

Karen Brooks thanks the following folks for their cooking secrets and magnanimous support: Ethel Fleishman, my mother and eternal soul mate, for always being there. Clara Eltman, for filling our house with laughter, love, and great music. Jodi Fleishman, my brightest star. David Estes, the Chicago kid and culinary wiz, and Susie Kitman, a sharpshooter of dead-on flavors, for inventive recipe testing and development. Victoria Frey, an extraordinary cook and friend, for constantly opening up her kitchen and heart. And to Peter and Julien Leitner, for making it all uproarious fun. Lisa Shara Hall and Sara Perry, for brainstorming, recipes, ideas, and being super pals. Len Reed, the enlightened poet-cook, who taught me the meaning of guy truth. Matt Kramer, who generously passed on some tenets of great cooking. For sharing prized recipes: Bruce Carey and Chris Israel of Zefiro restaurant and our friend Peter Sistrom. Tim Sills, whose wild, inspired energy runs throughout this book. And to my friends who always get me through the hard times: Susan Orlean, Trink Morimitsu, Ron Kogan, Joan Strouse, Marty Hughley, Shirley Kishiyama, Edward Taub, Patricia Allison, Ronni Olitsky, Gloria Spiritas, Mira Wilder, Ann Wall Frank, Roger Porter, the A&E gang, and Josie, Brad, and Ellis Stemple.

Gideon Bosker thanks the following friends who inspired recipes and offered perspicacious insights into the meaning of Dude Food: Chris Hubert, Hugh Van Dusen, Lena Lencek, William Galperin, Jack Watson, Tom Kuper, and Mittie Hellmich.
We'd also like to thank SuperStock for helping us with access to their wonderful image banks.